AF569528

KIDS BOOK OF VISUAL IDIOMS AND PHRASES, PART-1

A HANDY BOOK WITH IMAGES, MEANINGS AND EXAMPLES. FUN TO TEACH, FUN TO LEARN

PRACHITI K. SHARANGDHAR

Copyright © Prachiti K. Sharangdhar
All Rights Reserved.

This book has been published with all efforts taken to make the material error-free after the consent of the author. However, the author and the publisher do not assume and hereby disclaim any liability to any party for any loss, damage, or disruption caused by errors or omissions, whether such errors or omissions result from negligence, accident, or any other cause.

While every effort has been made to avoid any mistake or omission, this publication is being sold on the condition and understanding that neither the author nor the publishers or printers would be liable in any manner to any person by reason of any mistake or omission in this publication or for any action taken or omitted to be taken or advice rendered or accepted on the basis of this work. For any defect in printing or binding the publishers will be liable only to replace the defective copy by another copy of this work then available.

My Maternal Grandparents on their 50th Wedding Avnniversary

I want to dedicate this book to the two most important people in my life. They are my maternal grandparents. I would call them Aji (grandmother) and Pappa (grandfather). Through my childhood I had several learning related challenges. When everyone had lost hope, they had faith that I was capable of much more than what meets the eye. Their faith in me helped me overcome my learning related challenges and device my own unique methods for learning new concepts.

Thank you Aji and Pappa for your love and trust. It's because of your blessings that I have reached so far. Continue to shower your love from the skies above.

Contents

Contents

Quote

Teaching something new to children is essential, but, teaching in the right manner, matters the most.

-Prachiti Sharangdhar

Foreword

This book is a compilation of some firey idioms and their uncomplicated meanings. The simple yet brilliant examples for each idiom make learning easy-peasy for kids.

The exercise at the end of each chapter creates an opportunity for brainstorming and facilities out of the box thinking.

The pictures add visual appeal and are engaging. Each chapter enables interaction and discussion at multiple levels.

This book is a must-have for anyone who wants to introduce idioms to kids and improve their conversational skills.

- Siddharth Rajsekar (Founder: Internet Lifestyle Hub)

• • •

The 'Kids1st Books of Visual Idioms and Phrases' by Prachiti is clearly a work of a passionate teacher and a loving mom who understands a child's visual learning brain.

The way she has explained idioms using visual icons and metaphors not only gamifies learning but also helps in placing the idiom in the visual memory stack of a child's brain. It makes so much sense to offer teaching to students in a visual format even if it is about learning a language. After all, even when we read, we form an image in our mind.

Although this book is designed for kids, but I think it will also give teachers a thought to prepare their content in a visual manner. I am sure every kid who has this book will enjoy the experience and will not forget the idioms ever.

I wish Prachiti a great success for this book and eager to see more of your work in future.

Piyuesh Modi

Piyuesh Modi,
Visual Business Storyteller,
Netherlands

Preface

The Kids Book of Visual Idioms and Phrases-Part 1, is the first book of the series. In this book there are 15 idioms and Phrases. It is best for children in the age-group of five to 10 years. I've tried to incorporate some fun elements for the grown-ups also.

Benefits for children, parents and teachers.

- Simple language
- Easy to learn/ teach
- Can be used for playing games
- Excellent bed time read
- Improves the bonding
- Handy travel buddy
- Helps in improving recall
- Improves cognitive ability
- Enhances creativity and out of the box thinking
- Can be used for innovative games

This book is written in a workbook format. This means, after reading, there is an opportunity to apply the knowledge. Continue to read and you'll know how...

- The language is simple.
- The idioms are explained in a rebus format. This means a picture is used instead of the word. E.g., to depict up- one can show an arrow that is facing upward.
- The pattern or the style of the contents is as follows.
- The chapter of the idioms begins with a drawing or the pictorial depiction of the idiom or phrase.
- It is then followed by its name or what it is called.
- After that a simple explanation or meaning has been furnished.
- This is followed by 3 examples or sentences with the respective idiom or phrase.

- The fourth sentence is left blank for the parent or child to write (immediate pplication of knowledge).

Once all 15 idioms are over, there is a worksheet towards the end. It's a fun activity to understand if the child has understood all the idioms. The best practice would be to first complete all the 15 idioms and phrases, revise them and then discuss the worksheet. Again, it's absolutely ok if the child gets few or none correct.

There's a separate section on how to use this book. This includes various techniques that will help children develop reading habits.

Acknowledgements

I'm highly grateful to the Almighty for all the blessings.

Being a spiritually inclined person, I feel blessed to be a part of the Art of Living foundation and want to thank Guruji for his blessings and the whole AOL family. During some challenging times in my life, I received lot of love, help, healing and blessings from them. The Sudarshan Kriya, Mediation, Yoga and Pranayam have helpem become more confident, calm and have helped improve my focus.

Special thanks to my mentor Siddharth Rajsekar for helping me transition my coaching from offline to the online platform and introducing me to a whole new world of training and coaching. Under the guidance of Sidz (as we call him) I got an opportunity to learn from various international trainers. Its Sidz, who has inspired me to author a book. He has built a community – ILH (Internet Lifestyle Hub). A big thank you to all the members of this global community. Many of them have helped me in various ways. Some of them have become **friends for life.**

I learnt Visual Thinking from Piyuesh Modi and am grateful to him for sharing this knowledge with me. His course helped me in understanding how to simplify complex ideas and put them on paper with the help of simple sketches within a few minutes. I have applied the same knowledge in this book and have sketched various images. A handful of them are digital images. All the images, that are hand sketched are done by me. Book writing was not an easy task. I was stuck on few ideas for book writing and procrastinated for a long time. However, the visual thinking sketches helped me in completing all the hand sketched images in about 90 minutes **(ONLY)**. Thanks to Piyuesh who made it possible.

I can never thank enough the two most important men in my life:

My husband Karan Sharangdhar and my son Vivaan (he is 11 years old now). They always stand strong with me and support me for all my projects. Be it travelling for days or late-night webinars and training sessions at home. If I want to do it, they help me in making it happen. They are my pillars of strength.

My whole family and all my friends have encouraged me and have always shared an honest and constructive feedback. Their contribution cannot be explained in words. I'm grateful for having them in my life.

I want to specially acknowledge the contribution of all the trainers with whom I have worked on various projects. The list is endless.

My clients with whom I worked on various projects, special thanks to them. Working with all of them has helped me interact with people from various age-groups and backgrounds. All these experiences have exposed me to the different ways in which people learn new concepts.

Last but not the least, I want to thank all the Kiddies, kiddos, children, bacchas (children in Hindi language) and all the cuties with whom I have worked during my days as a preschool teacher. The have brought so much light and so many smiles in my life. It is because of them, that I am motivated to come up with this book.

Introduction

How to use this book for desired outcome

The idea of making a workshop style book really thrilled me. Imagine having a reading book that is a workbook and an excellent learning tool!!!

Pointers to keep in mind while reading this book.

1. Before starting with the reading exercise, its crucial to understand that children are not expected to understand the images and how they are linked in the first attempt. It may take few reading sessions for them to get used to the new concept.
2. Help the child identify the drawings, if unsuccessful, you can help and furnish clues or give answers. Just ensure, the child is not stressed. We don't want children running away when they hear idioms or phrases. LOL!!!
3. Help the child colour shapes or pictures with relevant colours, e.g. yellow for sun and hay. Pink for pigs, etc.
4. Once the child gets used to the idiom and is able to identify it, reward by giving a Hi Five or by any other fun action (avoid chocolates-we want to reward them in a fun way).
5. The idioms are written in small letters. Capitalization is not used as these are used somewhere in-between the sentences and normally not towards the beginning.
6. After the idiom has been identified, read its meaning and explain in simple words or in your mother tongue. The plus sign (+) is an indicator of separating words. Its should not be read aloud. In case the child reads it, its alright, eventually it should be explained that it is to separate different words.
7. **Use the pointer (index) finger of your right or left hand while reading.**
8. Start from reading word by word and move your finger under

each word that you are reading.

9. Don't expect that the child will start reading immediately. One may need to instil confidence in the child, therefore, give the child some time to read. Here Patience is the Key.
10. If the child is curious, let the child repeat after you. You read one or two words and move your finger along with the words, and the child repeats the same process after you. This will be really interesting.
11. Now, it's time for the examples. Here, explain to the child that the idiom will be used in sentences.
12. Read each sentence and explain the meaning. After few repetitions, eventually, the child can begin to explain the meaning in his or her own capacity and it will be fun to watch.
13. The last sentence has been left blank for you to fill. Either a parent can help the child to construct a sentence and write or the child can write on their own.
14. You can read two or three idioms every night before going to bed. Avoid rushing into finishing the book as it may cause confusion. It may be overload of information for the child. If the child insists to read more, can read without the expectation of learning everything in a few days.

Let this reading experience be more of an experiential learning rather than a reading marathon.
Have Fun...

CHAPTER I

What are idioms and phrases?

What is an idiom?

An idiom is a phrase, saying, or a group of words with a metaphorical (not literal) meaning, which has become accepted in common usage.

What is a Phrase:

A small group of words standing together as a conceptual unit, typically forming a component of a clause.

Importance of Idioms (and phrases) in English Language:

1. Idioms play an important role in the enrichment of the English language
2. They represent unique cultural and historical information
3. They broaden people's understanding of the English language
4. Idioms can make ones' speech more colourful and alive
5. Using idioms can highlight your speech and make it more impactful
6. Idioms can add emotions, vibrance, seriousness or curiosity to your message
7. They may not imply the literal meaning but a figurative one
8. Idioms are an important part of **all the languages** and are widely used to enhance the impact of the message.

Theories on idioms:

There are some theories that state that idioms cannot be one word, for e.g., Hot, hot has a literal meaning as well as it can mean something very popular or famous, like a hot topic. This means a topic that everyone's talking about. Some experts say that this means that hot has different meanings, that's all!!!

There are other theories that believe that compound words too can be called as idioms: e.g., moonlight- this means that one has a second job or secretly work in the night for extra money without anyone knowing about it. Other words are: Godspeed, horsepower, brainwash, brainstorm, etc.

On some information portals its mentioned: an idiom also means a form of expression natural to a language, person, or a group of people, therefore a single word idiom is acceptable to them

Basically, the discussion is ongoing...

There are mixed views on this topic.

Owing to social media, people easily post their views and long discussions crop up on various platforms. This makes it very challenging to understand from where the topic has originated. At the same time, one can keep the mind open to new ideas and build or create new knowledge based on the existing one.

Difference between Idioms and Phrases

Sr. No.	Idioms	Phrases
1	An idiom is an expression made by grouping words together to mean something that is different from the literal meaning	a phrase is a group of words used to define an expression
2	figurative expression giving meaning to a phrase or conversation	phrase can have a literal meaning

Q. Where can one use idioms and phrases?

A. Idioms and phrases can be used in many ways:

- In daily conversations
- While playing games
- While writing compositions/essays
- Prose or poetry

One can get creative and use them in jingles or songs also. It's all up to you. **Cool!!!** Isn't it?

CHAPTER II

Idiom 1: bed of Roses

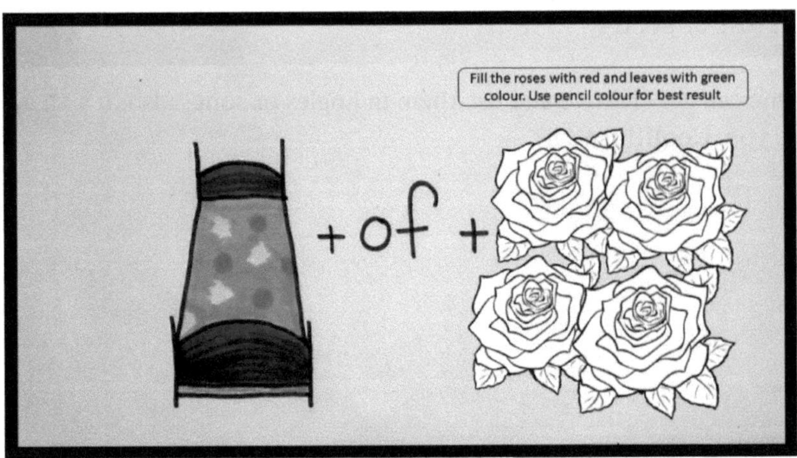

bed + of + roses

Meaning:

Very easy
An easy option
Something that can be done easily
Any task or activity that is very easy to perform

Example 1

Vivaan feels that dancing is like a **bed of roses**.

Example 2

Baking bread may look like a **bed of roses** but it's not.

Example 3

Do you think climbing a mountain is like a **bed of roses**?

Example 4 (your sentence or sentences)

CHAPTER III

Idiom 2: raining cats and dogs

raining + cats + and + dogs

Meaning:

Very heavy rains
Raining very heavily
Lots of rain pouring from the sky

Example 1

The school was closed as it was **raining cats and dogs**.

Example 2

The football match was cancelled as it was **raining cats and dogs**.

Example 3

Our garden was flooded as it was **raining cats and dogs**.

Example 4 (your sentence or sentences)

CHAPTER IV

Idiom 3: miss the Boat

miss + the + boat

Meaning:

Miss the chance
Lost the chance or did not win
Did not take the chance
Did not understand something

Example 1

It was a painting competition and Ashwin **missed his boat.**

Example 2

Dev had invited Tanvi for his birthday. She **missed the boat** as she was playing with her cat.

Example 3

We **missed the boat** of movie tickets as we were stuck in traffic.

Example 4 (your sentence or sentences)

CHAPTER V

Idiom 4: once in a blue moon

once + in + a + blue moon

Meaning:

Very rarely,
Not very often
Happens after a long time

Example 1

Shweta likes to go for shopping **once in a blue moon.**

Example 2

Aashvee throws tantrums **once in a blue moon**.

Example 3

The kids go to the beach **once in a blue moon**.

Example 4 (your sentence or sentences)

CHAPTER VI

Idiom 5: zip your lips

zip + your + lips

Meaning:

Be quiet,
Stop talking immediately

Example 1

The kids were supposed to **zip their lips** during the movie.

Example 2

All the guests **zipped their lips** as they were going to wish Shanay Happy Birthday.

Example 3

People must **zip their lips** near a patient, in a hospital.

Example 4 (your sentence or sentences)

CHAPTER VII

Idiom 6: piece of cake

piece + of + cake

Meaning:

Any action or task that is very easy to perform
Something that is easy to do

Example 1

Making a paper plane is like **a piece of cake**.

Example 2

Tenaz learns poems like **a piece of cake**.

Example 3

Aahana makes cooking look like **a piece of cake**.

Example 4 (your sentence or sentences)

CHAPTER VIII

Idiom 7: when pigs fly

when + pigs + fly

Meaning:

Impossible
Something that will never happen

Example 1

Chirag will keep quiet only **when pigs fly**.

Example 2

Aadya will stop hopping only **when pigs fly**.

Example 3

Calvin will clean his room **only when pigs fly**.

Example 4 (your sentence or sentences)

CHAPTER IX

Idiom 8: in hot water

in + hot + water

Meaning:

To be in trouble
Facing some problem
Feeling ashamed of some action

Example 1

Jiyansh was **in hot water** when his mother caught him playing online games.

Example 2

Reyansh was **in hot water** when his lie was caught.

Example 3

The kids were **in hot water** when they broke the glass.

Example 4 (your sentence or sentences)

CHAPTER X

Idiom 9: the other side of the coin

the + other + side +of +
the +

the + other + side + of + the + coin

Meaning:

The opposite view or argument
The opponents' side of story,
To look differently at one situation
Can also mean literally looking at the other side

Example 1

Swati got scolding for sleeping in the class, but the teacher did not look at **the other side**.

Example 2

Vaishali did not **look at the other side** when Vikas lost the game.

Example 3

We should look **at the other side of the coin** before making any judgement.

Example 4 (your sentence or sentences)

CHAPTER XI

Idiom 10: make hay while the sun shines

make + hay + while + the + sun shines

Meaning:

Do the work at the right time.
Perform any task when it's the right time to do it, don't delay.
Take up the opportunity when you have the time.

Example 1

Aarav told his mom that he wanted to study in his vacations. He wanted to **make hay while the sun shines.**

Example 2

The children **make hay while the sun shines** by enjoying all the delicious dishes during the festival season.

Example 3

Darsh **makes hay while the shines** by completing all his art projects on time.

Example 4 (your sentence or sentences)

CHAPTER XII

Idiom 11: busy as a beaver

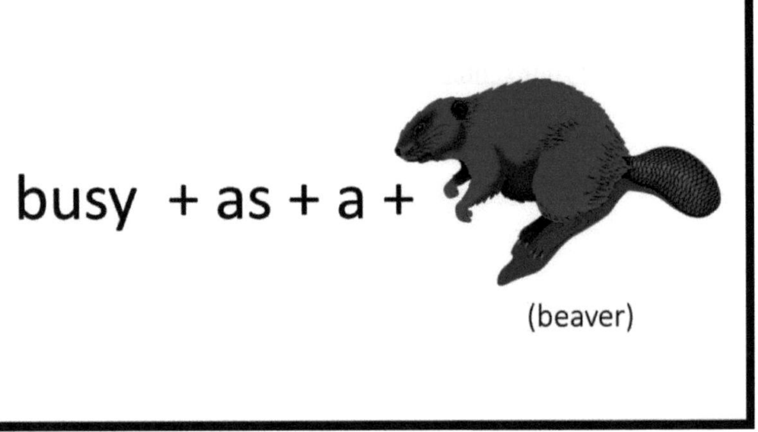

busy + as + a + beaver

Meaning:

Very busy
Working very hard
Working non-stop

Example 1

Diyaan is as **busy as a beaver** in the mornings.

Example 2

The teacher was **busy as a beaver** during the exams.

Example 3

Don't pretend to be **busy as a beaver**. I know you have nothing to do.

Example 4 (your sentence or sentences)

CHAPTER XIII

Idiom 13: hand in hand

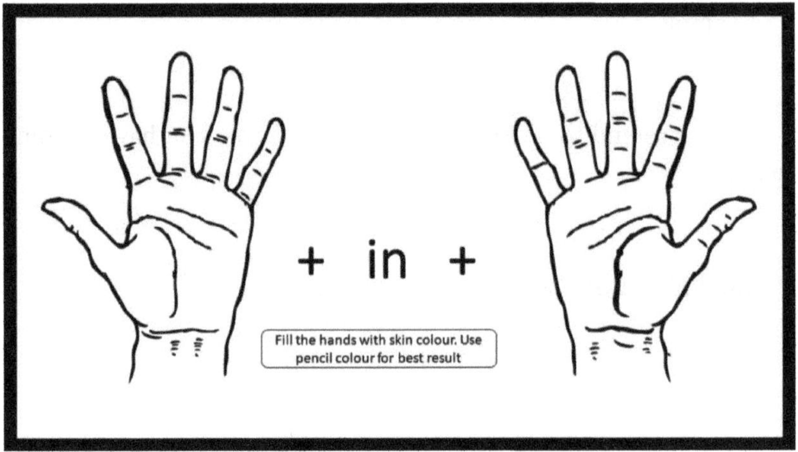

hand + in + hand

Meaning:

Work like a team.
Closely connected.
Holding hands.

Example 1

Puri and Bhaji go **hand in hand**.
* Puri (a type of Indian Bread)
* Bhaji (cooked vegetable)

Example 2

All children worked **hand in hand** for the craft project.

Example 3

Saurav and Joshua walked **hand in hand** while trekking.

Example 4 (your sentence or sentences)

CHAPTER XIV

Idiom 12: red zone

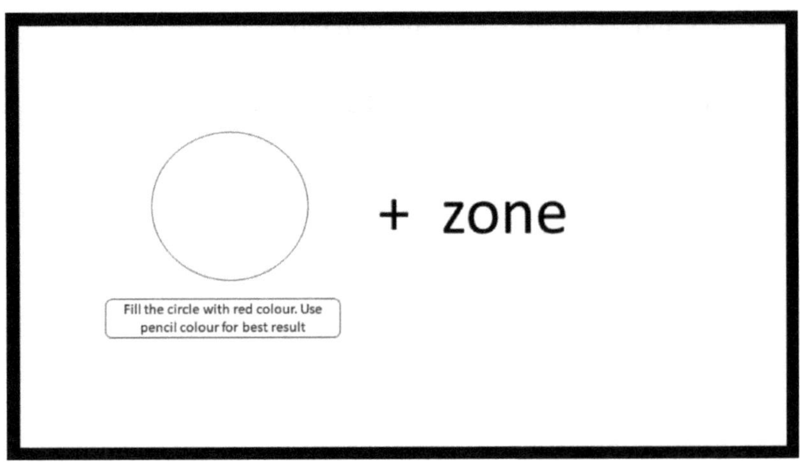

red + zone

Meaning:

An area on the map that is dangerous.
Any place that one must not enter.
Any area of army or military which is not open for all to enter.

Example 1

The kitchen becomes a **red zone** when my mother is cleaning it.

Example 2

During our vacation, we saw a board of **red zone** in the forest.

Example 3

Madhuri's house is a **red zone** during summer vacations. She has many guests visiting her.

Example 4 (your sentence or sentences)

CHAPTER XV

Idiom 14: upside down

upside down

Meaning:

Inverted position
Any activity that has not shown good result.
Any activity that did not happen as planned.
The result of the activity is exactly the opposite of what was planned.

Example 1

Vritti flipped **upside down** while dancing.

Example 2

Geeta's shopping plans went **upside down** when she had guests.

Example 3

Arjun's science project turned **upside down** when he used the wrong powder.

Example 4 (your sentence or sentences)

CHAPTER XVI

Idiom 15: deep-rooted

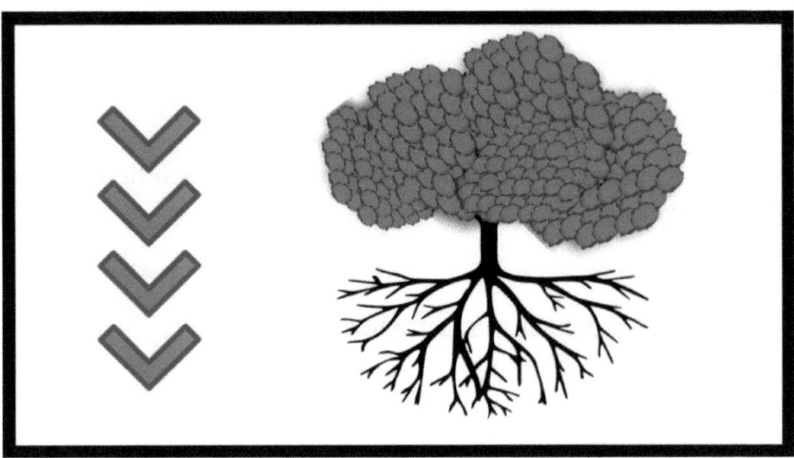

deep-rooted

Meaning:

Very strong idea that is difficult to change.

Some thoughts or ideas that people have been building in their minds for a long time.

Some habits that are in one's mind for long time that they are difficult to change.

Deep roots of a tree

Example 1

Ram won the student of the year award as good habits were **deep-rooted** in him.

Example 2

Ayaan's habit of disturbing the class was **deep-rooted**. The teacher had to work very hard to change it.

Example 3

This tree cannot be moved to another location as it is **deep-rooted** in the ground.

Example 4 (your sentence or sentences)

CHAPTER XVII

Idiom Test

Worksheet: Underline the idioms or phrases in the below sentences:

1. Movies and popcorn go hand in hand.
2. Krishna stays busy as a beaver by helping his friends in their studies.
3. Rehaan was in hot water when he was caught stealing.
4. Shravan cooked hot dosa pancakes for his family when it started raining cats and dogs.
5. The forest officer takes leave once in a blue moon.
6. Seher understands the other side of the coin before giving any judgement.
7. The phone fell upside down while removing from the bag.
8. The thief zipped his lips when the police officer caught him.
9. Handling a puppy is not like a bed of roses.
10. Ayesha will stop being naughty when pigs fly.
11. Lakshmi Amma stopped tourists from entering the red zone near her village.
12. Lord Hanuman had deep-rooted love for Lord Shri Ram.
13. The boy missed the boat of winning the essay competition.
14. Sarita didi cook's meals for 30 people every day. She makes cooking look like a piece of cake.
15. The busy father plays with his kids on weekends. He makes hay while the sun shines.

CHAPTER XVIII

A note of thanks

Thank you for investing your trust in me and reading this book.

I hope you enjoyed the experience of this unique workbook-like visual book. This book has been made by with over a decade of experience in education industry, 8 plus of years of experience in training and coaching and lots of research and sleepless nights. I have tried my best to simplify the concepts for educators to teach and for children to learn.

The teaching tips covered in this book are the tip of the iceberg. There are several other pointers that I have shared in my online courses which are available on my online school for teacher and parents. It called the Kinder Guardians Arcade. There are many courses that help Preschool parents and teachers to become impactful educators. You can visit my website **www.prachitisharangdhar.com** to know more about these.

I conduct free webinars and share many parenting and teaching tips. You can enrol for these webinars as well. There are special gifts for those who attend the whole session. I honour your time and try my best to give you value for any webinar that you attend. You can get all the details of my webinar from my website.

If you need any clarity, you can book a free, 30 minutes consulting session on my online calendar. During this session, we will discuss the challenges that you are facing as a teacher or a parent to pre-schooler.

If you have any constructive feedback or any inputs that will help me in improving the content for the other books in line, please share with me on **creative.expressionhub@gmail.com**

The next book (which is work-in-progress) is an extension of the current book. It will have other 15 idioms and their drawings and explanation with examples. I'm planning to add a chapter on games with idioms. This will have a list and rules of some creative games and activities that one can play with kids, the whole family or students. Hope you are equally eager to read it as I am to complete it.

If you have enjoyed this book and the purpose of having it is solved, do give a 5-star rating on the platform from which you have purchased, will be an excellent motivator for me. A positive review with a picture of your favourite page will be an incentive :)

CHAPTER XIX

Bibliography

Bibliography

Reference of idioms: www.theidioms.com

Difference between idioms and phrases: http://www.differencebetween.net/

Meaning and sentences: Internet search engine and personal experience and judgement.

Some Pictures: www.Pixabay.com

Hand drawn Sketches: I have sketched all the hand drawn images.

Epilogue

This short book has been created with a lot of hard work. It was written rather typed in 14 hours at a stretch. I was up almost whole of the night.

The reason was: My passion to get it on the floors ASAP. It was project that was waiting to happen from a long time. I had gone through several case studies of children who had learning issues and had worked with some of them to help them improve.

Starting with my son Vivaan, I was working with him from past few years. When he was in 1st standard, he came crying from school one day and refused to go to school the next day. On further probing, I got to know that he had got a zero in a dictation test and other children made fun of him.

I sat with him and had a long chat. I had to help him understand to accept failures and to try hard or bounce back. Although a chirpy child, he would get nervous to answer in class. He needed to develop confidence to answer even if it was wrong.

There were some unpleasant incidents with one of the teachers who would teach him. This made matters even more challenging.

After working with him for over two years and after having a lot of patience, there was a noticeable change in him. The change was gradual and happened over two years. Brick by brick.

Eventually, he developed confidence to interact with the school teachers and ask questions if he had any doubt. His studies score too improved. When I say improved, I don't mean 10 on 10. I mean he started understanding concepts and started enjoying appearing for tests with a calm mind.

Then there were other children with other behaviour and attitude challenges.

While traveling for conducting training in a school, I came across some students who never sat quietly in class and would distract others who paid attention.

I spoke with each and every one of them to understand the real reason behind their behaviour. Most of them were surprised as **I never punished them** but instead asked to meet them after class and discussed the challenges that they are facing.

The reasons behind their misconduct were as follows:

They were not very familiar with English

At home, the spoke in mother tongue

One student was orphaned

One had very strict parents

And the list goes on...

The root cause behind most of their behaviour issue was, that their basics were not clear and since they never understood English that well, they would get bored during any kind of training session and would land up disturbing others.

This happened in the year 2019- just before Covid-19 happened.

The lockdown game me ample of time to study and research and come up with some solutions.

This led me to create innovative teaching techniques and creative worksheets.

Ultimately the idea of writing a book that would help parents and teachers teach children intense or challenging concepts in a FUN way cropped up.

After writing three incomplete books, I finally thought, "what am I doing"? Also, I realized, that research and study are a never-ending process. Let me do something that really could create an impact. However small, its alright, but just do it :)

That's how with all the pent-up energy, I sat for typing the book and it was ready within a day.

Autobiography

Prachiti Sharangdhar

I would like to share with you something interesting about my childhood, School-to be more specific. It's important for me to share my true self and what challenges I faced in my growing up years, with you. No sugar coating. Life as it was!!!

If someone asked you to recall three memories from your school time, what would they be? Just think for a moment.

For me they are: my teachers yelling on me and calling me dumb, lazy and disinterested. Some teachers would fling my homework book on the floor. Yes! That was me and that's what some teachers thought of me.

Most of my teachers felt that I will never be able to do anything substantial or meaningful in life. In fact, I have a faint memory of one incident where one teacher told my parents that they should get me married as soon as I attain the marriageable age (during those days, the legal age was 18 years).

They felt that I was too dumb to understand studies and that nothing goes in my head. This was somewhere during the 1990's

Fast forward this to 2012: I had enrolled myself in a one-year course of Early Childhood Care and Education. During this course I got the opportunity to study child psychology an understand why children behave in a certain way, what could be going on in their minds, how they may interpret situations or actions and what impressions or marks, incidents leave on their fragile minds. It was then that I realized that I was a Special Ed. child.

Now what is this special ed?

In simple words, children who learn concepts in **different or unconventional ways** are called special ed children. For e.g., they can learn science concepts by playing games or maths concepts by measuring furniture in their house. I realized that the black board and chalk method did not work for me during my school days.

Rewind back to the 1990's: In school I would love to sit near the window and gaze outside. I would love the feel of the fresh breeze. The letters that the teacher would write on the black board seemed to dance. I could literally visualize that the symbols (answers) written on the board are dancing. I couldn't even identify the spot from where to read next when someone stopped reading before me. I would get all confused and it's no surprise that my exam scores were not at all decorated.

In the school I was a perfect introvert and a scared cat (in Hindi we say, Bheegi Billi). However, the other side of my personality that the school teachers were not aware was that I was a child theatre artist.

My first performance was when I was about two and a half years old. I wish I had that picture to share. Anyways, I could not learn a single answer, even if it was of two lines but I would easily by heart a whole drama script of 100 pages. I couldn't pick up the paragraph for reading but strangely I was able to remember dialogues of each and every actor. Outside the school I was confident, cheerful and surprisingly my uncles and aunts would call me smart. No one ever believed that I was weak in studies.

I was promoted to the 10th grade and had to live up to the expectations of my parents and the trust invested in my abilities by my teachers.

That was when something magical happened.

I devised my own way of learning concepts. After returning from school, daily, I would make diagrams of chapters (now we call them mind maps- I didn't know that at that time), draw some answers in the order of occurrence (flow charts or visual thinking), made jingles on theorems and postulates (now called- out of the box thinking). For the first time in my life, I was not nervous before my board(10th) exams. To everyone's amazement, I scored a first class. This was a **game changer** in my life.

I started teaching dance in the vacations of my 10th standard. From there on my school life changed drastically.

Dance class practice during the vacation of 10th Standard

In my 11th and 12th, I was in-charge of the cultural activities, started participating in sports and became the captain/ flag bearer of my group (yellow house) and led the whole group during the march past. In fact, my house got the award of the best performing house in the whole school. In an interschool drama competition, I got the award for the best actress, got an opportunity to represent school in elocution competitions and was actively involved in all cultural events of the school.

Annual Sports Day- Award for the best House

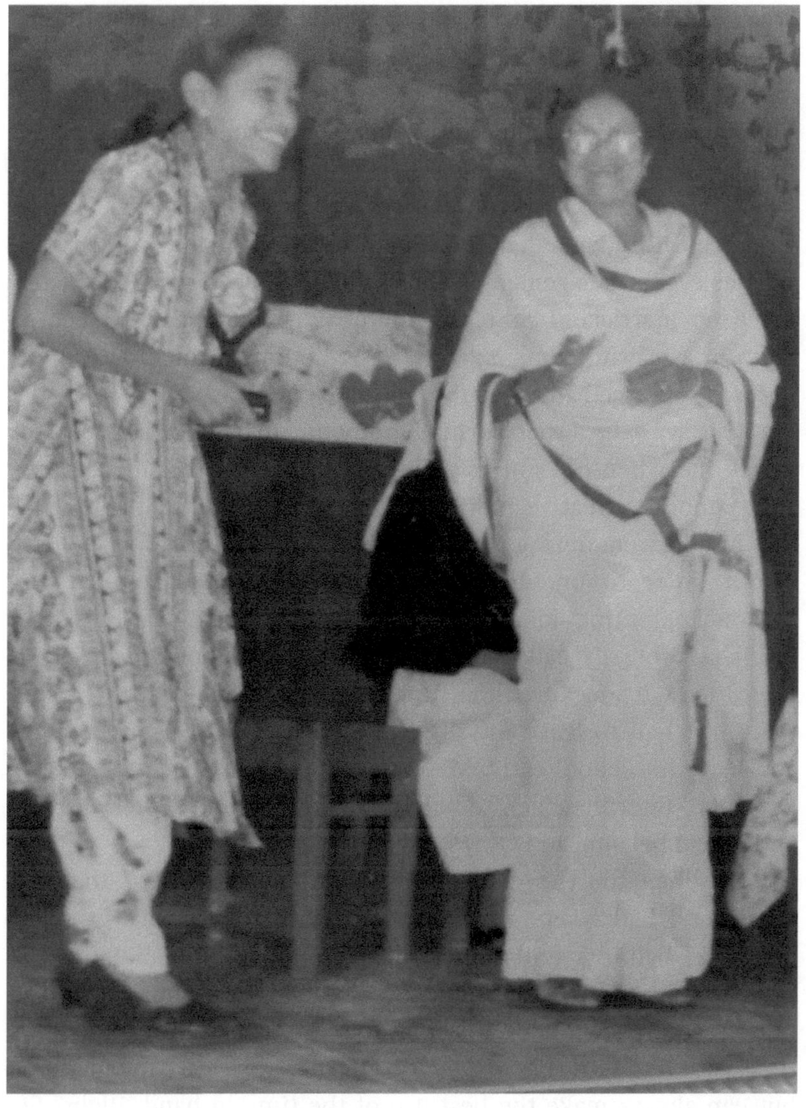

Received The Best Actress Award in an inter-school Drama Competition (12th std.)

After my 12th I started working with non-Government organizations in Vadodara (my birth place). So along with my college, I started community service and worked in many villages around the city. I even got invited to a school for judging a book summary recitation competition of students studying in secondary standard- I might have been hardly 17 or 18 years of age.

Post college, I worked as a free-lance event manager (now a days, we call independent working professional) and worked with various event management agencies and organizations.

After marriage, I shifted to Mumbai and immediately secured a job in a private company as a business development executive. Career progressed and then motherhood dawned.

This was the other **turning point** in my life. A sudden fear struck me when my son was born. I feared: What if his learning ability too was creative and what if he goes through a similar phase that I underwent during my school days?

In order to understand my child better and improve my personal parenting skills, I enrolled myself for a one-year Preschool teachers course called ECCE (Early Childhood Care and Education). It was an offline course and had a one-year internship too. So, I had to leave my little one (two year old at that time) and leave for school early. My day in the school would begin as a preschool intern teacher and after 12 p.m. I would switch my role and would become an ECCE student.

Enrolling for the course was undoubtedly one of the best decisions I had taken. Yes, it involved lots of sacrifices from my end and I had to spend a lot of sleepless nights in completing the projects and taking care of my son. Some social events too had to be missed. My son started seeing me less. I missed that bonding time with him (for that one year). One can never get the lost time but can always make the best use of the time in hand. Right? So, once I completed my course, my son was ready for his preschool.

He would go to school in the morning and I had taken up a job as a special ed teacher in another school.

After school hours, I would sit with my son and teach him songs, poems and many fun games. We bonded like best friends.

Well, I had the confidence and the skill to understand his learning requirements and work with him.

In the school I got to work with many special ed students. At the end of the academic year, 80% of them showed 95% improvement.

That was when I thought to reach out to a larger number of students and people and started conducting trainings.

Now, I have been in the education industry for over 10 years and a trainer and coach for over 8 years. In the last 8 years, I have coached over 8,000 plus participants from various age groups and educational and professional backgrounds.

I travel to different cities and conduct **train the trainer workshops** for the teachers. The best thing about my work is that I get to interact with so many people and observe their thinking, perceiving and learning patterns. I have an online school for parents and teachers. It is called, Kinder Guardians Arcade.

My Mission statement is: I am on a mission to help a 100,000 teachers and parents become educators to preschool students in the age group of 3 to 6 years of age.

With this mission I have created the online academy where, there are various courses for parents and teachers that will help them become better educators and develop a bond with their students or children.

I want to create a breakthrough in the Preschool teaching techniques and make children love studies. The preschool age is a foundation for the mainstream schooling. Therefore, its highly important to focus on how children enjoy learning rather than how much they learn.

That's the reason I have started writing books. This way, I can reach out to many Parents, teachers, educators, trainers and coaches and help them create that impact.

As this book is being published, the second one is already in the making. My books are interactive and they are created in a workbook style. I'm very passionate about what I do and dearly wish that no child should ever be negatively labelled or categorized by teachers or parents.

Let's make learning FUN for everyone. Thank you for joining me in my mission. Together we have a long way to go!!!

Answers To The Worksheet

Hope your test went well. Its ok if you got some wrong answers. It's important that you attempted the test

All the answers / Idioms and phrases have been underlined.

1. Movies and popcorn go hand in hand.
2. Krishna stays busy as a beaver by helping his friends in their studies.
3. Rehaan was in hot water when he was caught stealing.
4. Shravan cooked hot dosa pancakes for his family when it started raining cats and dogs.
5. The forest officer takes leave once in a blue moon.
6. Seher understands the other side of the coin before giving any judgement.
7. The phone fell upside down while removing from the bag.
8. The thief zipped his lips when the police officer caught him.
9. Handling a puppy is not like a bed of roses.
10. Ayesha will stop being naughty when pigs fly.
11. Lakshmi Amma stopped tourists from entering the red zone near her village.
12. Lord Hanuman had deep-rooted love for Lord Shri Ram.
13. The boy missed the boat of winning the essay competition.
14. Sarita didi cook's meals for 30 people every day. She makes cooking look like a piece of cake.
15. The busy father plays with his kids on weekends. He makes hay while the sun shines.

Printed by Libri Plureos GmbH in Hamburg, Germany